My Inaudible Whispers

Umang Mudgil

First Published in November 2020

ISBN: 978-93-5427-059-8

BLUEROSE PUBLISHERS
www.bluerosepublishers.com
info@bluerosepublishers.com
+91 8882 898 898

Cover Design:
Sanya Rastogi

Typographic Design:
Tanya Raj Upadhyay

Distributed by: BlueRose, Amazon, Flipkart, Shopclues

Dedicated to moose (massi)
(The strongest illumination of wisdom
and courage I have ever seen)

Preface

These Inaudible Whispers come deep down from my heart, each poem or tale written in this book will take the readers through a journey of ups and downs. These experiences are what I have felt dearly at some point of time in my life. The 20 years of my life are made to some use as I have gathered all the experiences adored by me in this book.

All the things left unsaid, all the whispers which were unheard are successfully recorded in this book.

Hope the readers can connect with the thoughts presented in the book.

About the Author

Umang Mudgil is from Ludhiana, Punjab. She completed her schooling from Sacred Heart Convent School, Ludhiana. She is a Microbiologist in becoming, studying at Panjab University Chandigarh. To skip her monotonous schedule of studying, She decided to follow her passion to write. She writes poems and writeups from daily life experiences. She can also be found painting the walls with colourful graffitis, She loves painting too.

You can follow her up on instagram handle

@the_inaudible.whispers

Acknowledgements

The inspiration which drove me to write this book is realization of self. Its the person within you who needs to stand up for your own self to make others believe in you. First of all I would like to lay my heart filled gratitude towards my pillars of support, my mother and father for their love towards me, and their faith and belief in me.

Secondly I am grateful to the team of Bluerose Publishers for making my dream of becoming a published writer come true. I would also like to thank all my family members and friends without whose support and assistance I would not have achieved victory over my dream project.

Lastly I would thank my bestest friend who stood by my side whether there was sun shining through bright skies or thunder and lighting shrieking through dark clouds.

Contents

POETRY

1. God's Wrath

God puts me to test now and then
By taking away one of them
He wants me to gather more strength
But all this leaves me more tense
Of all the odds, today he asked of you
And that could destroy me to pieces I knew
I cannot fight with destiny
All the wrath will still befall upon me
And I will be asking for plea
All that can be heard are screams
That just haunt my dreams
I cried, "Don't go!"
Because I don't know if there is a tomorrow

2. Misunderstood

I maybe misunderstood
But things are not always how they look
Because inside and outside are two
different outlooks
I am neither wrong nor right I
am what makes me fright
Although I may sound stupid
But my life isn't that lucid

3. The one who elopes

Till how long will you hide in your cape?

Till how long will you escape?

You knew the end was near

And now it couldn't pass one more year

Go tell them on your own

That it isn't your throne

You didn't deserve it

Go -admit it

It was all a lie

When you looked them through their eye

You aren't the one

Whom they imagined as the sun

You aren't the hope,

But you are the one who eloped

4. Celebrating love

Weak people target others
Because they are scared many
could do wonders
The strong shouldn't fear them
As they aren't the real gems
Keep building your castle high
up in the skies
But these weak wont be able
to rise
But you my darling, would stand
up high above
Embracing all others with your love
Keep doing that for all
Celebrate love more than anyone's
fall
Nobody is others
We all together are brothers

5. A fairy tale

Through the dark night
The princess sat by the window
Awaiting her knight
The lush green gardens were
covered with snow
In the wintery breeze
He came up to the door
And bent onto his knees
Oh my my I thought it happens
in fairy tales
But alas! I was woken up by the
sound of the rails

6. Go with the flow

Winds blow
Colours show
In times of trouble people go
Today is there
Tomorrow might not be
So go with the flow

7. She

She is like the sun
Either could give you warmth
And save you from the storms
Or her red flashes
Could burn you to ashes

8. On your side

With just one person on your side
You can stand out with pride
All the rough times pass in seconds
And when you are with them it feels
like heavens

9. My first and last teacher

My mother taught me everything

I'd do

From my first breath to my first step

From my last step until my last breath

My first and my last teacher -MOM

10. Mother

From the times you held my tender hands
To guide me through the pebbled lands
All this time you stood by my side
Prevented me from every tide
I will love you till my last breath
Because you my mom, you are worth
every second until my death

11. All black

Love in my eyes
Faith in my soul
I still stand there holding hope
That one day you will realize
You broke the rope
That held our bond
Which we have gone beyond
Now nothing stays the same
There is no picture in the frame
As everything has burned down to flames
It took me sometime to forgive you
But now you've showed me the true view
Now I don't get any flashbacks
Because you've turned them all black

12. You & me

There is no need to moan
For I have left the throne
I don't own, all this alone
You know me, for what
I have shown
But my dark sides will
still remain unknown
For now I have gone
Don't wait for me until dawn
I have taken away with me
All the beautiful memories
of you and me

13. Phoenix

God puts me down
He wants me to drown
So that I become stronger
and take up the crown
He makes me fall
So that in my eyes
I seem small
He does that with a motive
So that I remain devoted
Devoted towards my purpose on earth
That I have carried along since my birth
So owing to all this I put away my sorrow
And start my planning for tomorrow
I like a phoenix
Will rise from my own ashes
To win the prize
And win through all the crashes
Yes I will
My life hence will remain no
longer still

14. Caught between a delusional war

Sometimes I ponder
My hopes grow fonder
I think about my
purpose on earth
That I have carried
along since birth
What am I born for ?
Cause I am caught
between a delusional war
Whether to go right or left
Or just stand in the centre and rest
I question myself
"Was I born to be good or bad ?"
If I'd get the answers I'll be glad
Am I the beauty or the beast ?
Tell me O'priest
Let me know for what am I alive?
Cause anytime my death can arrive

15. Virtual

Your appearance was deceptive
You looked so heavenly from
my perspective
But who knew you were a unicorn
You on the outside were full of colours
And never seemed like others
But who knew you would poison me with
you sugar coated sweetened candy and
then I realized there never existed a we

16. My hero

The hand you laid on my forehead
the time I was born
Is always a security that nothing
can go wrong
You are the pride I walk with
All dads are they same you have
proved is a myth
Whenever you see danger around
me you are ready
Like branches of tree so huge
and heavy
Your arms curl around me
And make me nostalgic about
the joys of childhood which
were carefree
I look up to you with gleaming eyes
Finding answers to all my
questions as a wise advice
You have been by my side
through all my sorrows and pain

And never given me a chance to complain
Till your hands rests above my head
My dear dad., nothing can stop me
from moving ahead

17. Fearless

She was laughed at
But she never cried about that
She was looked down upon
As if people questioning, "Why is she born?"
She wanted to run away
So that she doesn't become
another prey
She wanted to be freed
From the shackles of creed
As those ropes could strangle her
A coffin ready to get rid of her
And then all this would seem something
that could never occur
She was still
Full of will
She never left her determination
As she awaited for a train at the station
Saying a goodbye
To all those who kept an eye and

wanted to make sure that she dies

She was one of her kind

And strong enough to leave

them all behind

18. Survival

Cuddled inside the soft feathers
he felt safe
As there can be nothing compared
to a mothers cape
Discovering the newness around him
he tried to balance on those tiny legs,
he would stumble then fall and start again
Trying to adapt to the survival theory
of Darwin he would hide under his
mother, during times of trouble
But was all this enough to live?
The greedy and cruel world all around
Would eat up his innocence in one round
And then a thump was heard, gleamy eyes,
big paws, a creature way too big for him
jumped over
Utter darkness was all that could be seen
Yes, time got over for him way too soon
When he had just hatched out from his cocoon
The mother who was left behind

Was way too kind

Couldn't bear the loss

Crying and shouting in her own sound

Flew away forever to escape the chaos

19. Numbness

The clock ticks eight
I lay numb on my bed
My stomach hurts because
of the last night's food I ate
I have got pain in my head
which further makes me feel
as if I am dead
Ping! The phone on the bedside rings
But I don't feel any strength in my limbs
My mind reminds me of the pending tasks
But that wasn't enough for me to get up at last
All I want is to lay aimless
And I wish to visit the places
which are nameless
Because I want to rest for sometime
As I am tired of trying to make everything rhyme

20. I am strong

I am fierce and strong
Since the day you left me torn
But breaking apart was easy than
The journey I had begun
My inner self refused to fall
Because I had to live upon the
example I had set for all
I slowly gathered my pieces together
To finish up all my endeavours
Although my soul was broken
My body was frozen
My eyes were an ocean of emotions
But life was still in motion
Putting it all aside
I packed the bundle of lies
And started my journey to
a place from where I would rise

21. A second chance

A feeling of fear shakes me up
And my heart begins to jump
When I think of those hands
which held mine
So that's I walk through life's
different lines
Today when I stand alone
And think of you not being my own
Because of a mistake
Which you made
Couldn't it all get erased?
Cause I don't want someone's else
standing at your place
I feel your absence in my soul
That has created a major hole
I feel lost
I wish the limit wasn't ever crossed
Because my heart wants you to come back
Although my mind cant forget how
you turned my world black

22. Unsaid

My eyes are still
Looking at the window sill
I want to turn around and speak
About the things which don't let me sleep
But my lips are bolted in silence
Trying to maintain the balance
The dilemma whether to speak
up or not crowds my mind
Or should I just sit blind?
I left it all aside
And started to work till night
Finally I lay on my bed
Deciding that some things are
better left unsaid

23. Who

I didn't ever get a glimpse of you
My ears haven't ever heard you
My skin hasn't ever felt your touch
Your footsteps aren't heard much
Yet I can feel you all around me
Caressing my hair while I am
having tea
I know the old rocking chair rocks
in the midnight
But you are nowhere in sight
I search for you in dark dwellings
People think I am storytelling
Due to my strong desire to find you
Everything around me feels like a déjà vu
You have made me fall into a maze
From which I cannot get out even after so
many days
Trying to find you by all my ways
I haven't seen the sun blaze
The search for you will come to a climax
When one day I'll find the maps
Containing all the facts

24. Justice

If there as any justice in the world
I wouldn't find a sight so dreadful,
Of a small boy in torn clothes sitting
down the lane
To fill his stomach counting the grains
The girl in my neighbourhood wouldn't
bother about what to wear
She could roam courageously without any fear
The beautiful shine of the dark skin wouldn't have to hide itself
In order to prevent to be called a curse himself
The poor child wouldn't stand and stare the wealthy
If he himself was healthy
The love of two souls would find its way to be justified
By breaking all the barriers we are made to define
If such a world would prevail
Then ideas of justice would pervade
Then there will be no one to blame
You and I would be the same
Golden tears of joy would roll down our eyes
And there will be no one who hides in disguise

25. Timeless

The trees shed their orange leavers in the autumn
In November the flowers once again blossom
The day loses its sunshine
When the clock strikes nine
The moon pulls with itself the waves along the coastline
The stars seem to scintillate with a dark blue light
And add charm to the darkness of night
The hands of the wall clock keep on rotating
As if the time is accelerating
Although everything is in motion
You and me still have constant emotions
Although the sky keeps changing its hues from
orangish red to bright blue
We will always remain me and you
The bond we share is timeless
Without which there only exists silence

26. My brother

In the serenity of summer afternoon
I reminisce the time spent in 2012 June
During those carefree days
You and I would endlessly play
From cycling in the rain , to freezing
homemade candies and ice creams
We were an unbreakable team
Despite being shouted at
We were full of our mischievous acts
Although we fight a lot
But what we share is tied by an
imperishable knot
There was a time when my hands
reached till your head and I could smack you
but time just flew and you
I wish , you achieve colossal heights
And experience all delights
But for me you will always remain my little brother
For whom I'll always provide a cover

MICRO TALES

1. Trust

The whole world accused her for marrying him
"He would land you in trouble", they said
Years later she smiled from behind the curtains
As she saw her little tiny tot holding his
finger and going down the lane

2. Love

"It's raining hard maybe I wont come to school today"

she hung up

Who knew he stood there with an umbrella outside waiting for her to come

3. Friendship

Although he had done his homework this time

A notebook sneaked beneath the desk

He sat waiting for her to come and complete it for him

4. Eyes

That day our eyes confessed
Our lips said words which weren't heard
Our eyes heard voices of our brain
Our hands although still but seemed as
if in motion holding on to each other's
Our feet though still but seemed as
if approaching towards each other
All the world around through in motion
seemed still as if the only two beings
existent was us
That very day our eyes confessed

5. Inheritance

Scratched her head, bit her nails, she used to sit down on the table, a coffee mug placed right beside her, her pen clicking as she thought, she used to start to write as soon as something would strike, she would keep on working until night

Though she didn't make it up to the years

Eighteen years later

A brown haired, sixteen year old, bitting her nails, sat on the same table with the same coffee mug, filling page by page, seeming as if a born writer. Who knew she was one, inheritance and genes laughed from inside her

6. Dead bond

People who used to cling onto each other, be best of friends, share each and every small detail of day to day life, who used be just a call away -that's what you call best friends

Now they just text on birthdays

Who knew a lie could hold so much power that it could separate a bond so strong

7. Final goodbye

Two decades back I laid my head in your lap
Those soft fingers ran through my baby hair
As you used to sing me a lullaby
Today your head rested in my lap
I touched your cold forehead with my bare hands
Just to say a final goodbye

8. Left

After you left

Even the funniest jokes and hilarious instances couldn't pull-up a smile on a face which used to beam with laughter on hearing the most ridiculous and stupidest things while you were beside

QUOTES

The feeling that once felt like glitters
Was now something that turned bitter.

After a few years.....
She: Why do you hate me still?
He: Cause maybe hatred is the strongest form of love.

Not a single tear could carry
The weight of lies I had been told.

Her face had a magnificent smile but the photo on the wall told a different story that all of it lasted for awhile.

Sometimes the beautiful outsides are broken insides.

If I lose you, I lose me.

My scars are so deep, That I didn't weep.

The wound you left me never fills even
after taking hundred pills.

You pushed me away until my world
turned grey.

You saw in me what I couldn't see for myself,
the real me

The parts of you in me feel as if you
never left.

Is it true, The butterflies in my stomach
danced around for the wrong person
all along ?

Your are the poem, That runs my heart.

You made me fall more every time
I looked at you.

Friends with paws, Will never land
you in loss.

Poetry is handful of words joined
together by emotions

I am the poet and you are my poem

Flowers are lovely and so are you.
If I'd loved you I'd never take away
your hue.

Are you a curse ? Cause you excite the
devil inside me.

The more you kept digging for the keys
to my heart the more I kept chaining
the locks.

If eyes speak, Then words stand meaningless.

Those times were good when you heard my name
and smiled.
Today hearing my name could make you cry
What will hearing my story make you do ?

You are the heaven my heart feels and
my eyes see.

What you are to me is the same as what closed
doors are to a claustrophobic person.

You helped me dive into the deep waters
where I lose the sight of you.

My dreams are so bizarre cause in them
I fall like a soulless body.

As a small child my grandma used to tell
me the dead shine above our heads as
stars, I wonder then what runs behind
me in darkness.

Even a hurricane can't rob me of
memories of you.

The cold night in winters were meant
for stealing kisses while the traffic lights
flickered our faces.

Standing behind you made me realize
you only kept me in the shadows.

Your fragrance which can be smelt
even today when I pass by your empty
room keeps you alive in me.

She is a flower whose fragrance can
spread to far away lands even if you
wrap her petals in a box.

I want to rest for sometime as I am
tired of trying to make everything rhyme.

If I hold onto tears that doesn't mean
they aren't heavy

I still dream of the rainbow of memories that
bloomed once

www.ingramcontent.com/pod-product-compliance
Ingram Content Group UK Ltd.
Pitfield, Milton Keynes, MK11 3LW, UK
UKHW042000190726
13854UKWH00005B/2085

9 789354 270598